TRAINING TO SUCCEED

Tennis

Edward Way

FRANKLIN WATTS
LONDON • SYDNEY

First published in 2009 by
Franklin Watts
338 Euston Road
London NW1 3BH

Franklin Watts Australia
Level 17/207 Kent Street
Sydney NSW 2000

Series editor: Sarah Peutrill
Art director: Jonathan Hair

Series designed and created for Franklin Watts by Storeybooks.
Designer: Rita Storey
Editor: Nicola Edwards
Photography: Tudor Photography, Banbury (unless otherwise stated)

Picture credits
© 2003 Getty Images p7, © 2006 Getty Images p27, © 2007 Getty Images p26. Every attempt has been made to clear copyright. Should there be any inadvertent omission please apply to the publisher for rectification.

Thanks to Lindsay and Tim for all their help and to Sutton Tennis Academy (www.suttontennisacademy.com) for the use of their facilities. Also thanks to Jodie, David and Joe for their participation in the book.

A CIP catalogue record for this book is available from the British Library.

Dewey classification: 796.342
ISBN: 978 0 7496 8499 0

Printed in China

Franklin Watts is a division of Hachette Children's Books, an Hachette UK company.
www.hachette.co.uk

Contents

Me and my sport

Tennis is an exciting racket sport in which individual players (singles) or pairs of players (doubles) hit a tennis ball around a court. Points are scored by hitting winners or forcing opponents into making mistakes. At its pinnacle, tennis is a glamorous sport in which the top professional players are paid large sums to compete in worldwide tournaments.

Below the top tier of tennis, there are hundreds of young players hoping to make the grade and join the professional tennis tours. In this book, three talented young tennis players, who all train at Sutton Tennis Academy near London, will share their experiences with you. They will tell you all about their training regime, their work on and off the court with their coach and the demands and challenges of competing in their sport.

David stretches to play an overhead shot. He is wearing mainly white clothing, which is required at some tennis clubs.

Jodie Williams

Jodie is 17 years old. She comes from Nottingham, although she is living and training in London full-time. She recently went on a seven-week trip to Africa where she played Futures tournaments to add to her **WTA** (Women's Tennis Association) ranking. Away from tennis, her hobbies include shopping, going to the cinema and playing guitar.

I used to play a lot of sports for the school, like netball, athletics, badminton and football. It wasn't until I was about ten that I started going to my local tennis club for a weekly session with a coach and other players. From that, I gradually started playing more and more because I loved it so much. It's a great feeling when you know you've played well or done the best you can.

David Johnson

A former highly-ranked table tennis player, David Johnson is 16 years old. He finished 2007 as the number five ranked under-15 player in Britain, and the following year was a finalist or winner at three different junior grand prix tournaments.

I took up tennis at the age of 12. At first it started out as one of my activities at school, but it later developed into a deeper passion for the sport. The size of the tennis court was a factor – it was vastly bigger than a table tennis table. I could hit a wider variety of shots and I could also use more of my athleticism by covering the court and retrieving difficult balls.

Joe Salisbury

Joe is 17 years old and a winner of Tennis Europe events in singles and doubles. In 2007, he was chosen to hand a tennis racket, signed by the Davis Cup team, to the Queen at the opening of the National Tennis Centre in Roehampton, London.

I started playing tennis when I was four. My mum used to be a tennis coach and I played other sports as well but I preferred tennis. It's an individual sport which makes it a bigger test and it also gives you greater satisfaction when you succeed, because it is only you that has done it. Tennis is also a test of every part of yourself – the mental, physical and tactical sides, as well as pure talent.

David, Joe and Jodie shake hands at the net after a game of mixed doubles. Tennis is a highly competitive sport, but players always respect their opponents.

Starting out

Millions of children have played tennis for fun on courts at school or in a park. Frequently, the next step up is to play for a school team or to join a tennis club with a juniors section. If players show talent and improve, they may get the chance to play in local tennis tournaments. Success there can lead to appearances at bigger competitions and, potentially, the first thoughts of making tennis a career.

I began playing tennis at school by first playing in the PE sessions and attending the training sessions after school and at the weekends. I later joined my local tennis club and soon after started playing competitive matches in the inter-club and county tournaments.

I remember my first international match. It was in France when I was about 12. I was very nervous but I think that helped me play well. I did not have any pressure on me so I did not have anything to lose. I can just remember being really excited and looking forward to it.

Tennis clothing

Tennis clothing (a shirt and shorts for male players and a tennis dress or a shirt and shorts or a skirt for female players) should be comfortable and not restrict your body's movements. Shoes are the most crucial part of a player's clothing. Dedicated tennis shoes offer grip on the court and support the foot and ankle as a player moves sideways as well as backwards and forwards.

My first competitive match was a long time ago now, but it was at Nottinghamshire County Closed Under-12s. I remember feeling nervous before the match because I was unsure as to what would happen, but when I started playing my competitiveness came out and all I wanted to do was win.

Jodie takes her tracksuit top off before playing. A tracksuit helps keep a player warm before and after training or matches.

My parents encouraged me to play tennis to start with because they said it was a good way to make friends when we moved towns. But I soon started loving it so much, I was the one pushing myself and they supported me greatly. I knew as soon as I started playing that I wanted to play tennis more than anything else, and I just carried on feeling that way.

My first competitive matches were when my mum entered me in mini tennis tournaments. Mini tennis helped me because I would have been too small to play proper tennis, so it gave me a chance to play at a young age.

Starting out schemes

Mini tennis and other schemes for very young players feature smaller courts, balls that are easier to control and simpler rules. They offer an excellent way into learning some of the core skills involved in tennis, including watching a ball's path, moving to meet the ball and basic shots on the **forehand** and **backhand** side (see page 11).

Coach's notes: starting to compete

In Britain, young players may be introduced to competitive tennis through fun match play and internal club matches. Eventually, they may be able to obtain an LTA (Lawn Tennis Association) ranking, which will enable them to play in LTA-sanctioned events.

Joe moves quickly into position so that he can play a shot on his backhand side. Learning to time the shot so that the racket meets the ball well only comes with a lot of practice.

Training and practice

Talent will only take you so far. Young tennis players who want to succeed have to back their talent with large amounts of intense training. Players train most days of the week when they are not playing tournaments. Their training mixes work on shot techniques, movement and tactics, with tough fitness training to build their strength, speed and flexibility.

In the gym

Tennis players train under the close eye of a specialist fitness coach. Each player will usually have his or her own dedicated fitness plan which will have a number of goals. These plans include a series of short, sharp drills to build the players' speed and their ability to change direction quickly.

Joe finishes a backhand shot in training with a powerful follow-through. Shot practice and time on court will make up more than half of Joe's training time.

I train every day except Sunday. I play for four hours a day and do two hours of fitness. I most enjoy playing different point situations and doing drills where I can work on things that need to be improved in my game. At the end I feel a little bit more confident in that particular shot or situation.

I train five to six days a week. Each day usually includes about three hours of tennis and two hours of fitness. I warm up in the morning with the fitness trainer for about half an hour, then play tennis for two hours, then do an hour of fitness exercises. Sometimes it's the same in the afternoon. Usually, I do drills in the morning and play points in the afternoon. Fitness work is focused on endurance, speed, flexibility or strength.

Jodie lifts a weights bar in the gym, watched by a fitness trainer.

David performs some sit-up exercises as part of his training to build his abdomen muscles.

As young players, they are seeking to improve their overall strength and their core stability – the strength of their body's core muscles – which will help to give them a firm base from which to work. They are also seeking to build up their fitness levels and to increase their **stamina** – the ability to perform at a high level for longer periods. Fatigue in the latter stages of a match is often a major cause of a drop in a player's performance.

The players build their speed and stamina in the gym using a treadmill.

*I most enjoy the match-play tennis training sessions as I am extremely competitive and just love winning. I least like the fitness sessions, especially endurance speed tests such as 'the **bleep test**' or treadmill and bike exercises, as I find them very boring and tiring.*

Working with my coach

Coaches are crucial in the development of young tennis players. They can not only improve players' individual shots, but work on all aspects of their game – from overseeing their fitness training, to learning and appreciating the tactical side of tennis.

Meet the coach: Tim Webster

Tim Webster is 26 years old and began playing tennis at the age of two! He has played in national and international tournaments and was ranked within the top 40 players in Britain. As well as being a coach at the Sutton Tennis Academy, he still plays in the National Club League (his team are the current champions). He works closely with his players to improve their fitness, speed, stamina and shot skills, as well as their mental strength and their use of tactics. One of his mottos to his players is, "train as you play, play as you train".

My coach definitely helps me with my mental game. Little things, such as what to do in between points and at the end of games to keep focused, are key and my coach helps me plan a routine for this.

My coach is very encouraging and hard-working. I get on well with him. He makes me work hard and get things right. We also have fun. He has helped every part of my game.

Tim works with Joe on his service action (see p14-15). He is encouraging Joe to bend his arm at the elbow a little more to help with a smooth swing.

Tim gives Jodie some advice on playing a two-handed backhand shot. He leads her through the foot positioning and the movement of her body and arms.

*Jodie reaches to play a forehand **volley** (a shot made before the ball has bounced) during a drill organised by the coach. He has a large basket of balls with which to keep feeding the player at the other end of the court.*

Making adjustments

A coach is in the perfect position to spot small yet important flaws in players' movements, or in their technique when hitting a particular type of shot. Tim explains any problems he identifies to the players, and then suggests ways in which they can improve. These are often based on making small adjustments, which are then reinforced through regular drills and exercises.

Tim uses a video recorder to capture the movement of players as they make a shot. He can run these back in slow motion, pause to highlight an error or improvement and compare them to footage of leading professionals.

If my coach sees anything that needs to be improved, he will tell me what needs to be done and we will do what's best to make the improvement. For example, he changed my backhand technique because I kept hitting the ball late. So he made me shorten my backswing and hit through the ball more. We did a lot of basket feeding to help me learn this technique.

Playing shots

Tennis is a sport of quick movement and sharp decision-making and tactics. But most of all it is about playing good, accurate shots, also known as strokes. Players spend a lot of time working on a variety of different shots to groove their action so they can play them well throughout a match. Players who are confident of hitting a wide range of different shots are better equipped to handle whatever their opponent throws at them.

*David plays a powerful forehand groundstroke. His racket has come over the top of the ball to generate **topspin**. This means that the ball will dip after it has travelled over the net.*

Different shots

Shots are sometimes split into those played on the forehand side (the side of your body that has the hand that holds the racket) and those on the backhand side. The backhand drive, a common shot in tennis, can be played with one or two hands gripping the racket. Tennis shots can also be divided into **groundstrokes** (shots hit after the ball has bounced on your side of the court), and volleys which are hit while the ball is in mid-air.

When hitting volleys near the net, always have your racket head above your wrist, bend your knees more as the ball gets lower, contact the ball in front of your body and hit through it.

To hit a good shot, I would say your positioning is probably the most important thing. You may have the best technique in the world, but without the footwork your shot will not be as impressive as you expect. It's very important to keep your eyes focused on the ball. This may sound silly and obvious, but a lot of the time players do not give 100% concentration to tracking the ball and therefore can end up being in an incorrect or awkward position to hit the ball back.

Drills and thrills

Most shots training is split into two parts – drills and points or match play. A coach may organise a series of shot drills – exercises where the player repeats the same shot in the same situation. This can help reinforce a new tip or a change in technique that the player is learning. Match or points play is where the player puts the new tip or shot technique to the test in a simulated match situation or by playing real tennis points.

The players perform a drill in which they receive the ball hit from the coach and hit a strong groundstroke back. They aim for the ball to land in a narrow corridor between the sideline and a green cone. Drills like this can help hone the accuracy of a player's shots.

My forehand is my favourite shot because I can use it as a weapon. I don't usually spend time on specific shots; I do everything in a training session. I sometimes practise at the weekend away from my coaches.

Coach's notes: making shots

*One of the main factors of good shot-making is to make sure you have a wide base and a low **centre of gravity** before, during and after your racket hits the ball. Practice is also an essential factor in making the shot every time.*

Serving and receiving

Every point in tennis begins with one player serving the ball from behind the baseline. The server aims to send the ball over the net and into the service box diagonally-opposite. A serve can be a potent weapon, allowing a player to win many straightforward points. However, if players struggle with their serve, it can also be a major weakness which their opponents will seek to exploit. This is why players spend plenty of time practising their service action, grooving the movements so they can repeat them under pressure.

I practise my serve by serving out a trolley of balls one after each other in quick succession. By repeating the service action, I can improve my serve consistency, accuracy, spin and power.

You generally aim for one of three places with your serve: out wide, into the body of your opponent or down the 'T' (the middle of the court). In matches, you try to serve to where the opponent's weakest shot is and where you are most likely to get an easier first ground shot.

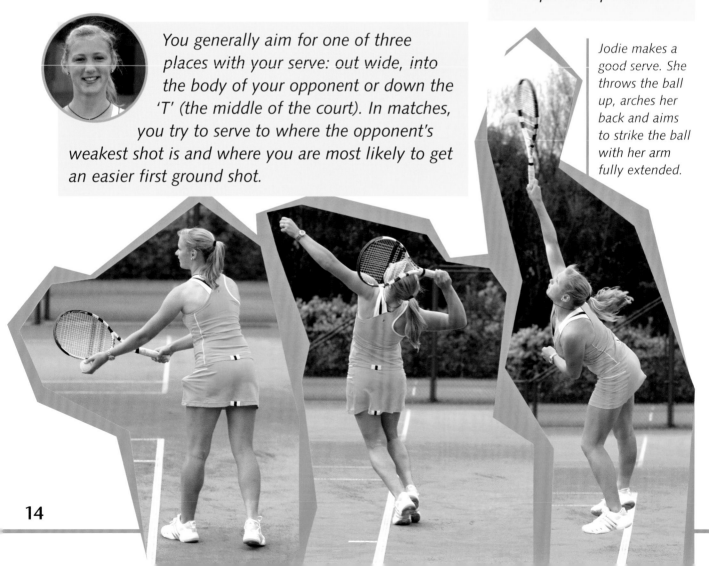

Jodie makes a good serve. She throws the ball up, arches her back and aims to strike the ball with her arm fully extended.

David works with his coach to ensure that he has a good receiving position. He is balanced with his weight equally on both feet. He holds his racket out in front, ready for a serve to his backhand or forehand side.

Coach's notes: receiving serve

Keep your eye on the ball the whole time and take up a court position that allows you to cover both sides of the service box. If the serve is fast, move back, and if it is slow, move forward. Early preparation is key. Do whatever you can to put the ball back in court.

First and second serves

Players have two chances to serve each point. If their first serve doesn't clear the net or fails to land inside the correct service box, it is a **fault** and players make a second serve. Good servers try to send the ball where their opponents least want it, pressuring them and making their **return** shots as short and weak as possible. Hitting a particularly fast or well-angled serve may mean that the receiver misses it altogether – this is known as an **ace**.

Even if players prefer to hit their serves into one place on the court, many players mix up the positioning of their serves to keep their opponents guessing.

Receiving serve

The first thought in a receiver's mind is to reach the serve and return it so that it is in play. If a serve is short or weak, a receiver can aim to do more, hitting a strong return that may win the point.

When receiving, I will change my returning position, depending on factors such as my opponent's service angle and pace. For example, if the opponent is able to serve far out wide, I will stand more into the tramlines to be able to cover the serve. Similarly, if the opponent's serve is not that fast, I may stand further in the court towards the service line to attack the serve and reduce the time my opponent has to react.

On-court tactics

Tennis is a highly tactical game. Players must be fit, fast and have good shots. Even so, if they aren't able to think their way around the court and make good judgements on where and when to play the right type of shot, they will struggle.

Forward or back

Some players are serve-volleyers, preferring to sprint in behind their serve in the hope of getting an easy volley to put away for a point. Other players are more content to stay at the baseline, playing longer **rallies** and hoping to find an opening or exploit an opponent's weakness to score points.

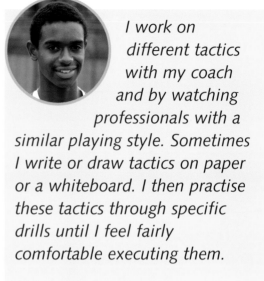

I work on different tactics with my coach and by watching professionals with a similar playing style. Sometimes I write or draw tactics on paper or a whiteboard. I then practise these tactics through specific drills until I feel fairly comfortable executing them.

When in trouble during a point, I mainly try and hit high and deep into the middle of the court to give myself time to get back to the centre of the court. If my opponent is at the net, I will try to hit it to their feet or try to pass them.

I try to mix it up and sometimes serve and volley and sometimes stay at the baseline. This stops the opponent hitting the same return every time.

Jodie runs in hard to reach a short ball played by her opponent. She reacts quickly, so that with a good sprint she will be able to return the ball.

*Joe has disguised what sort of shot he intended to play before making a short, **drop shot**. The ball just creeps over the net, will only bounce very gently and may not be reachable by his opponent.*

Players may choose to alter their game depending on the opponent and the court conditions. Courts can be made of clay, grass or carpet, and there are different types of hard court, too. Each surface can play differently.

My favourite surface is either indoor hard or carpet as it is extremely fast. I am more of a baseline player, as I like to hit hard groundstrokes. However, usually my style of play results in a lot of short balls played by my opponent, and so I do not hesitate to capitalise on these and come into the net to finish off the point.

I tend to stay at the baseline, but if the ball is short I will attack and come to the net. My favourite surfaces are hard courts but I don't really have a least favourite, although I find clay a lot tougher because it's slower so the points last a lot longer!

Coach's notes: preparation

Remember to think about your strengths and how best you can use them. Try to use all the things you know about your opponent to your advantage. Use their weaknesses against them and do your best to stop them using their strengths.

Setbacks and sacrifices

Playing tennis competitively is exciting, and for some players rewarding, but it can come at a cost. Players have to give up a lot of their free time and make other sacrifices as well to achieve the most that they can. They may also encounter setbacks, such as a loss of form or a disappointing series of losses. For young players who are eager to learn and play, it can be extremely hard to deal with an injury or illness.

Injuries are definitely the worst part of playing tennis. Even when the injury has fully recovered (if it does properly) it takes a long time to get back to the same standard as you were before and to compete at the same level. My worst injuries have been my ankle (I tore two ligaments) and my back (scans discovered I had three stress fractures in my back). I was out for a year and have been playing properly now for a few months, although I still get a few problems with my back.

Competitive tennis demands full commitment from young players. There is a heavy workload of training and competing, with much travelling in between. This all has to be fitted in around schoolwork, which leaves relatively little time for socialising or pursuing other interests.

I had glandular fever and could not play between September 2007 and June 2008. I'm still trying to recover my fitness now but I have to be careful not to do too much because it is easy to get ill again. It was very frustrating not being able to play.

Jodie performs an exercise designed to help strengthen her back so that she can put everything into her serve and other shots, and not fear pain or a recurrence of her old injury.

Joe and David sit down at their training centre's canteen to eat some fruit and cereal bars.

Players also have to be disciplined in their lifestyle which includes eating healthily and keeping fatty, sugary fast foods to a minimum.

Coach's notes: eating well

Carbohydrates and proteins are an important part of a player's diet, so players eat lots of pasta the night before a match, and bananas and cereals leading up to a match. Also, chicken and fish are both foods that are high in protein, so we encourage players to eat something like that the night before a match too.

I personally do not have any regrets, because sport is a huge part of my life, and being able to play it almost daily gives me great enjoyment. Tennis does obviously take up some of your leisure time, and as a result I cannot chill out with my mates as much as I would like to, but I have a big network of friends in and out of tennis.

When suffering from setbacks, many players find it helps to talk over their problems with other players they know as friends, or with their coach.

I do not have a lot of time to do anything apart from my training and my schoolwork. I have to cut back on my leisure time to fit everything in. Although my training is not relaxing, it is very enjoyable. Even when things are not going so well, I still think the sacrifices are worthwhile because I enjoy it so much.

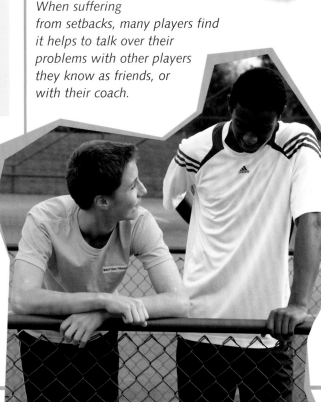

Preparing for matches

For these young players, the tennis season runs throughout the year, including indoor matches during the winter. If they stay fit, they may play 100 or more competitive matches per year. How do they prepare for each encounter? How do they stay relaxed yet get their bodies and minds ready for the challenge ahead?

Preparation starts as soon as you know when or who you're playing. I try to find out as much as I can about my opponent, if I don't already know her. Then in practice I will train the way I need to play her. I tend to practise for 30–45 minutes before a morning match. If the match is in the afternoon, I probably practise for longer.

My typical warm-up routine would be to do five minutes of aerobic exercises, such as jogging and side-steps, followed by five minutes of dynamic stretching. I would stretch my quadriceps, my calves, hamstrings, ankles, biceps, triceps, forearms, shoulders, hips and my back.

The players perform some high-stepping knee raises across the court as part of their warm-up procedure. Warming up and stretching is important before heavy training as well as before a competitive match.

I will run and then do some stretching and speed exercises. I have to stretch a lot because I am growing so it is easy to get injured, but there is nothing specific that I do. I listen to music and warm up on my own. I sometimes talk to my coach and then I warm up outside.

Joe plays a shot during the **knock-up** before a match begins. Good players use this time carefully to select which shots they want to practise and take note of how the surface is playing and the general court conditions.

Preparing for matches

In the minutes before being called out on court, players find different ways to relax in the locker room, from checking their equipment to listening to their favourite music. Big match nerves are common amongst even the best players and some are superstitious or follow the same routine before each game. Out on court, players usually spend five minutes playing shots to one another to ease themselves into the game.

I'm not superstitious, but I do like to do things the same way because I find routine helps me. I get a little bit nervous but more of an excited nervous.
During the knock-up, I work on timing the ball well and not making mistakes. This gets me into the right rhythm for the match.

David and Joe are in the locker room shortly before a match. This is the time to stay relaxed and focus on a game plan and match tactics.

In competition

Out on court, the match starts with a player either serving or receiving. Players try to hold their serve whilst seeking to break their opponent's. No two tennis matches are alike, and how a player adapts to the challenges ahead will play a major part in whether he or she wins or loses.

Tennis matches are usually the best of three or five sets with players winning a set when they have won six or seven games and are two games ahead of their opponent. A match can be over in less than an hour whilst many may continue for two, three or more hours of intense action. Although there are regular short breaks, a match can race by. Throughout a match, players need to assess coolly how they and their opponent are playing and what changes in their play they may need to make in order to win.

It is very important to break back immediately after losing your serve as, by doing this, you will stop any momentum that your opponent would have otherwise had. Momentum is a big factor in tennis, and if momentum swings your way you are likely to win the current game or set and possibly even the match just because of it.

Jodie has tracked the ball well and is in a good position to hit a powerful forehand drive.

David makes a powerful overhead smash. Played when an opponent's shot sends the ball high and short, a smash is hit with power but needs to be well directed to win the point.

Even if you know a bit about your opponent before the match, they may be doing things differently on the day, so you can learn a lot in the first few games. If you see your opponent is hitting one shot badly, then you can try to make him play that shot a lot.

Early on, I try to find my rhythm and range and see how the opponent is playing. I try to analyse which shots they are playing better or not so well, and where the majority of their shots and serves go.

Pressure points

Pressure mounts as a match progresses. Many tennis matches hinge on a small number of crucial points. These can include some **break points** in which, if the serving player loses the next point, he or she will lose the game, or set point, where one player has the chance to win the set. How a player responds after suffering a break of serve can determine the course of the set or the entire match.

David and Joe talk as they walk back to start the next point in a doubles match. Pairs encourage, support and communicate with each other throughout a match and may change their positioning and tactics to counter the opposition.

Building experience

Tennis players help build their experience by reflecting on a match after it is complete. They will often discuss how the match went with their coach, who may alter training or introduce new drills as a result.

Putting things right

Losses happen. Sometimes, players come up against inspired opponents, get some unlucky ball bounces or simply do not perform at their best. They may also have made the wrong tactical decisions or found that certain of their shots were not successful when they were put under pressure. Working out key mistakes and problems in their play can give players valuable pointers for the future and highlight the areas of

I've learned that a lot of the times when I come back in a match it is not because the tennis has changed, but because of something mentally. If you lose the momentum it is hard to get it back. One point can change a match because you can get more confident and your opponent can get upset or distracted by something.

Do I think about a match after it's over? Yes, for a while after. My coach tends to leave it an hour after my match has finished to talk so that all the emotions from the match settle. That way you can think about it calmly.

Joe makes a serve during training. How he has served in recent matches will determine what sorts of serves he works on with his coach.

When playing a European Tennis Association tournament in the UK, I lost in the first round of my age group, which was highly unexpected. I did not feel confident hitting the majority of my shots and most importantly I was not able to play in my usual aggressive style. During the break from tennis (for exams) beforehand, I'd forgotten my aim of staying close to the baseline and stepping into the shots therefore transferring my bodyweight into the shot, but was simply using my arm to produce the power.

their game they need to work especially hard on. Analysing a match you didn't expect to lose can be painful, but it can also lead to positive benefits.

Reflect on success

Most coaches urge young players to put just as much thought into analysing matches that they win. There may still be errors to identify or lessons to learn from their success, such as a particular shot or tactic that could be applied to future matches.

Coach's notes: reflecting and improving

Within every tennis player's career they will face poor performances and disappointing losses, but it is important to reflect on such situations to identify areas for improvement and draw positives, however small they may be, from the situation.

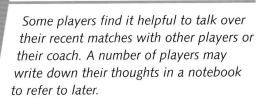

Some players find it helpful to talk over their recent matches with other players or their coach. A number of players may write down their thoughts in a notebook to refer to later.

My heroes

The sport of tennis has generated many star players over the decades, from legends such as Bjorn Borg and Martina Navratilova to current champions such as Venus and Serena Williams and rising stars like Andy Murray. Many of these top tennis players become heroes to younger players as well as to tennis spectators.

Jelena Jankovic watches the ball after playing a shot against Venus Williams. Jankovic became the world number one ranked female player in October 2008.

Tim Henman was my first hero because he was the first player I ever saw on TV when I was younger and he was the British number one. Today, my heroes are Rafael Nadal and Jelena Jankovic. I met Nadal in Arangi Park at Wimbledon once before he was about to practise. I had a picture with him and only spoke briefly, but he seemed so genuinely nice.

Every time I step onto the match court, I always think of Rafael Nadal and how he fights and gives 100% effort for every single point. I try to emulate this as much as possible within all my matches, as I believe it to be a very important factor. Many tennis players at a young age will find it hard to concentrate throughout the whole match. If you are able to do this, you can give yourself a big advantage.

I admire Andy Murray as he is very dedicated to improving and being the best at what he does. He inspires me through his recent increased fitness schedule and as a result he achieved some brilliant results, when before his fitness used to let him down. I admire Rafael Nadal for his physical endurance and strength which allows him to play in the relentless way that he does.

My first hero was Roger Federer. I liked the style of game he played and I aspired to play like that. I think that my game style is quite similar to his now. Also he is so strong mentally and never let his emotions affect him on court. He has been my favourite player since he won his first Wimbledon.

Learning from champions

Some tennis players do more than just admire their tennis heroes. They seek actively to follow or copy some part of their play or preparation. It might be their use of a particular shot or the dedication with which they train. Alternatively, some choose to follow part of their hero's attitude or personality which has helped make that player a great champion.

Andy Murray congratulates Rafael Nadal after losing to him at the quarter finals of the 2008 Wimbledon men's singles. Murray learned from the defeat and came back to beat Nadal at the US Open only months later.

Taking the next step

Few sports are as competitive as tennis throughout its many different junior and senior levels. Players cannot afford to let up or they face the danger of being overtaken by many other young rivals.

Players and their coaches will often set targets or goals. Some of these may be short term and about results to be reached in the next few months or current season. Others may be longer-term career aims or skills-based goals, such as improving a particular type of serve.

David turns away from the net and punches the air after winning a training match. David hopes to win many matches in tournaments to rise up through the ranks to compete at the highest level.

The next skill that I wish to improve is my **slice** *and slice return. Similar to Roger Federer, I prefer to return serves on my backhand side with a slice, however my slice is not yet good enough to do this – it can sometimes lack pace and be too high. I am currently working on this by returning all balls on my backhand side in training and match-play sessions with a slice.*

I need to improve my speed and strength to be able to hurt my opponents more. The most important thing for me now is physical work. I was ill for about a year so I lost all of my fitness and also awareness of the court. Once I have improved my fitness and play some more matches, then I think my tennis will improve greatly.

I need to improve consistency on my backhand and second serve. I will do this by practising a lot on those shots and also concentrating and working very hard.

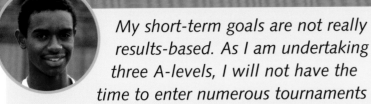

My short-term goals are not really results-based. As I am undertaking three A-levels, I will not have the time to enter numerous tournaments around the year. Instead, I am focusing on my level of play and I am setting goals to be of a certain standard after the end of each year. I want to be around the same standard as the top five players in the UK of my age group.

I want to get a women's world ranking as this is my last year of juniors. In the future, I want to be injury free and still enjoying playing as much as I am now.

Joining the professional ranks

As many talented young players progress, their thoughts may turn to leaving juniors tennis behind and competing with adults, potentially at full professional level. There are a number of pathways towards this goal, but all involve playing and succeeding in tournaments against equally or higher-ranked players. Rankings vary between countries and age levels and can be complex. They are essentially calculated from results obtained and the quality of the tournament and the opposition.

*In the next year I will start to play some futures events to try and get a ranking. In the future, I would like to be playing tournaments and travelling around the world and improving my ranking. Then I would like to be a professional on the **ATP** circuit.*

At professional level, common entry points are the futures events on the **ITF** men's and women's circuit. Succeeding here can mean that players obtain a world ranking which, if they continue to do well, may allow them to break into the main professional tours – the ATP for men and the WTA for women.

David, Jodie and Joe talk about their hopes for the future.

Glossary

ace A serve that is not even touched by the opponent.

ATP Short for the Association of Tennis Professionals, this is the leading tour for adult male tennis players.

backhand A shot hit from the side of the body opposite the racket.

baseline The back line of the court, which shows the court's length.

bleep test An endurance running test where players run between two markers (placed a distance of around 25 metres apart). The player must reach the second marker before a bleep sounds. As the test progresses, the time between beeps gets quicker. If you do not make it to the line before the beep then you have to drop out.

break To win a game when you are receiving your opponent's serve.

break point When the receiving player is one point away from making a break of the opponent's serve.

centre of gravity The point at which a body's weight is equally balanced.

coach The person responsible for training and supporting tennis players.

drop shot A soft shot that just drops over the net, falling short into the opponent's court.

fault A service that fails to place the ball into the correct area of play, therefore not starting the point.

forehand A shot hit from the side of the racket.

groundstroke A shot hit, often from around the baseline, after the ball has bounced.

ITF Short for the International Tennis Federation, this is the organisation that runs world tennis and organises the Davis and Fed Cups.

knock-up The period of practice between opponents just before a match starts.

rally A series of shots between players during a point.

return After the serve, any shot that has successfully passed over the net and into play.

service box The area on the other side of the net in which a serve must land in order to be legal.

slice To put a spin on the ball so that it travels in a different direction.

stamina The ability to maintain physical effort over an extended period of time.

topspin Hitting over the top of the ball to make it spin forward and dip.

volley Playing the ball in the air before it bounces.

WTA Short for Women's Tennis Association, this is the leading tour for adult female tennis players.

Find out more about tennis

Books and DVDs

Know Your Sport: Tennis – Clive Gifford (Franklin Watts, 2007)
Lots of information about tennis, with step-by-step photographs of some of the strokes as well as profiles and information about some of the world's greatest tennis players.

Inside Sport: Tennis – Clive Gifford (Wayland, 2008)
An exciting and instructive spectator's guide to the sport and how it is played.

Junior Tennis – Mark Vale (Hamlyn, 2002)
A truly excellent guide to playing tennis produced in association with the Lawn Tennis Association.

Complete Conditioning for Tennis – Paul Roetert and Todd S. Ellenbecker (Human Kinetics Ltd. 2007)
A book and DVD package containing many drills and exercises to improve a player's fitness and performance.

Tennis Skills: The Player's Guide – Tom Sadzeck (Firefly Books, 2008).
A solid introduction to the shots, tactics and skills needed to play tennis successfully.

Women's Tennis Tactics – Rob Antoun (Human Kinetics Europe Ltd. 2007)
Written by a respected women's tennis coach, this is a very informative guide to tactics used in the women's game.

A Champions Mind: Lessons from A Life in Tennis – Pete Sampras (Potter Style, 2008).
Sampras was one of tennis's greatest-ever champions and in this autobiography you learn about his mental toughness and dedication.

Wimbledon The 2008 Mens Final - Nadal vs Federer (Target DVD, 2008)
Need to feel inspired? Watch the epic four hours and 48 minutes of the 2008 Wimbledon Men's Final between Roger Federer and Rafael Nadal, one of the greatest-ever tennis matches.

Websites

www.itftennis.com
The official website of the International Tennis Federation, the body that organises world tennis. The website contains news of tournaments all over the world and lots of features on rules, training and other aspects of the sport.

www.atptennis.com
The ATP is the men's professional tour and this official website contains much information both on players, their rankings and performances, and the various tournaments in which they take part.

www.sonyericssonwtatour.com
The official website of the women's elite professional tennis tour contains competition news and profiles of leading players.

www.lta.org.uk
The Lawn Tennis Association runs tennis in the UK and its website is packed full of news, tournament schedules and other features on all levels of British tennis.

www.juniortennis.com
An interesting site on junior tennis tournaments, coaches and events. It also has a number of free articles on coaching, sports science and preparation before a match.

www.expert-tennis-tips.com/tennis-links.html
There are dozens of really useful links to other websites at this website, which is run by former Wimbledon Men's singles finalist, Chris Lewis.

Note to parents and teachers: Every effort has been made by the Publishers to ensure that these websites are suitable for children, that they are of the highest educational value, and that they contain no inappropriate or offensive material. However, because of the nature of the Internet, it is impossible to guarantee that the contents of these sites will not be altered. We strongly advise that Internet access is supervised by a responsible adult.

Index